16.95

W9-AWL-738

First published by Hodder Wayland
338 Euston Road, London NW1 3BH, United Kingdom
Hodder Wayland is an imprint of Hodder Children's
Books, a division of Hodder Headline Limited.
This edition published under license from Hodder
Children's Books. All rights reserved.

Series concept and design by Liz Black
Book design by Jane Hawkins
Edited by Katie Orchard
Science consultant: Dr. Carol Ballard

Published in the United States by
Smart Apple Media
1980 Lookout Drive
North Mankato, Minnesota 56003

Library of Congress Cataloging-in-Publication Data

Godwin, Sam.
    It all makes sense / by Sam Godwin. p. cm. – (Little bees)
        Summary: An introduction to the senses of sight, hearing,
        smell, taste, and touch.
            1. Senses and sensation – Juvenile literature.
            [1. Senses and sensation.]
            I. Title.
            II. Series.

        ISBN 1-58340-223-3

        QP434 .G63 2002   612.8 – dc21   2002023110

        9 8 7 6 5 4 3 2 1

It All Makes Sense!

A first look at the senses

buzzᶻᶻ

It All Makes Sense!
A first look at the senses

Sam Godwin

A+

Smart Apple Media

We have five senses to help us explore our world.

Come on, dear—let's fly. There's so much to see and hear!

And smell and taste and feel...

6

7

8

9

13

15

Our noses help us to pick up smells.

Some things smell nice...

18

19

21

We can feel the world around us by touch.

Stone is very hard to sit on!

25

And some things feel cold or warm.

Brrr! This water feels very cold.

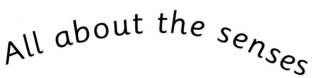
All about the senses

We use all our senses at once when we eat an apple:

We see the bright color of the apple.

We feel the smooth skin with our fingers.

We taste the sweet flavor of the apple.

We smell the aroma
as we peel the apple.

Useful Words

Aroma
A pleasant smell.

Bitter
A sharp, strong taste.

Nectar
A sugary substance made by plants to attract insects. Bees make honey from it.

Sour
An acid taste, like lemon or vinegar.

We hear ourselves chewing as we eat the apple. Yum, yum!